I0468049

Table of Contents

Legal Disclaimer

Forward

Thank you for purchasing the Low Cost J.U.S.T. Series Volume 1 – The 3 Step Essential Process When Starting A New Business

This J.U.S.T. series book was extracted from Low Cost Empire Volume 1— An Entrepreneurial Textbook. The focus of this J.U.S.T. series book is what to do when you think you have come up with a good business name or a good product name.

We want you to be sure that you do in fact have a unique name before you make any attempt to lock it down and spend hard earned money. If you did in fact come up with a great name that will ultimately be the identity of your company, we want you to be in a position to capitalize on it.

So, get ready to explore a routine that will serve you again and again for each new venture you do.

NOTE: Low Cost Empire Volume 1 – An Entrepreneurial Textbook, Low Cost Empire – Getting Down To Business – Filing your first Trademark, and **Low Cost Empire Volume 5 -- Getting Ready For Investors** goes over Patents, Trademarks, Copyrights, and shows you how to build a company in stealth mode. These books may be of interest to you in their entirety.

Let's get ready to examine the 3 step process.

Louis.

LOW COST EMPIRE J.U.S.T. SERIES

Just Understanding Specific Topics

VOLUME 1

**THE 3 STEP ESSENTIAL PROCESS
WHEN STARTING A NEW BUSINESS**

A NEW IDEA IS BORN!

Thank you for purchasing **The 3 Step Essential Process When Starting a New Business**. The essence of this booklet is basically an extraction from the Low Cost Empire Volume 1 which is a thorough and much larger multi-faceted book. This extraction with some new and unique material, will help you to focus on **3 items** that **must** be part of your decision making process at the very beginning of your venture. Once you know it, you can use it again and again for each new business idea. Okay, so you have a basic concept for a new business. There are a lot of pieces to the puzzle and there are a number of things to think about in terms of strategy. This booklet will go over **three items in particular** that must be checked before you move forward full force. We believe that in light of the different things that have to be considered, one does not have to go for broke. We also feel that being *unaware* of all of the resources available to you when starting a business contributes to the overall impression that it may be something that is out of reach. For example, a common misconception is that it is difficult and expensive to start a business when in fact you can save thousands of dollars by just understanding some easy concepts and doing certain initial steps yourself. Together, we will go over these three items that need to be considered. We think that this initial check list will serve you well in any business that you are considering.

Some of you reading this booklet might say "what about the business plan?" We do recommend you do a business plan. We just don't think it should be the total focus of this booklet. The subject of the business plan is a book unto itself. There is tons of help and explanation over the net. If you go to www.Score.org and go to **Business Tools**, they offer a very good business plan. Business plans are good for helping you to **focus and clarify** what you bring to the table in contrast with comparable, already established businesses. How is your product or service better than what others in your industry are currently offering? It also helps you to focus on initial expenses that will be needed. Courses and books that are devoted to centering around the business plan tend to be grooming their readers for a *traditional mom and pop* operation rather than thinking globally. Therefore, the focus of this booklet is to maximize your concept and reach of your business. We believe this is a "did I cover all of the initial questions pertaining to a new business concept name" kind of booklet. So, without further delay let's just get right into it.

Concept

One of the most exciting things you can do is to come up with a great concept and then go about the process of naming it! It is a lot of fun, but before you get too happy, you have to make sure that you really did just come up with a unique name. There are three things to do **simultaneously** in order to make a proper assessment as to whether to move forward with that concept name:

1.   Step 1: Check whether the **proposed** name has been already **trademarked** by someone else. **Go to USPTO.gov**. Go to **Search Trademarks** and use the **New User search**. But keep in mind that you need to be thorough.

Under **Trademarks** TRADEMARKS go to "Search and then Use the "**New User Search**".

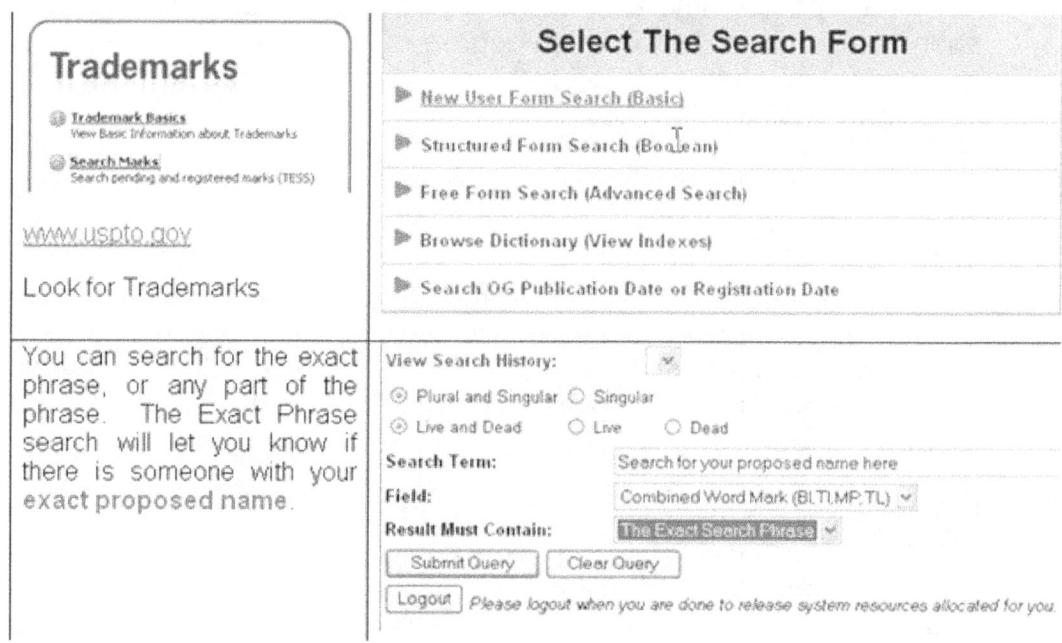

2. Now, if there is a match, check to see whether it is a "**live**" or "**dead**" filing. A dead filing simply means that the former owner did not file the appropriate documents and/or pay the required fees to maintain the trademark for whatever reason, and decided to **abandon** the trademark.

	Serial Number	Reg. Number	Word Mark	Check Status	Live/Dead
1	79072385	3767723	COOL SUN	TSDR	LIVE
2	78272320	3159750	COOL SUN REFLECTOR	TSDR	LIVE
3	78414299	3074543	TAN ESSENTIAL THE COOL SUN	TSDR	LIVE
4	75289446	2235134	COOL SUN...	TSDR	LIVE
5	75220257	2275158	COOL SUN...	TSDR	LIVE

3. If it is a **dead filing**, you do not have to worry. The dead filings are marks that have been **abandoned** due to lapse of fees or the owner simply lost interest. If the search comes up with "**no hits**" then you can be sure to a high degree of certainty that the name is available for trademark protection. You can file on-line for a trademark by following the instructions carefully

4. **If your initial search comes up clean (meaning no matches) then do the following.** Search for any words of your proposed mark and see what comes up. Search for different uses or spellings such as **Car Fax** or **Kar Fax** or **Kids World** or **Kidz world (Example of Pseudo marks)**. Be as thorough as you can as a non-legal professional. If your name is for example **The World Group** search it out for **World Group, Our World Group, World Group Leaders etc.** Don't just get excited because there was not an initial direct hit.

5. **Take your time and be thorough.** If another filing is in the system, whether it be Pending **(TM)** or Registered ® the Trademark Examiner can determine that your particular filing is **a bit too close** to the already existing filing and can **reject** your application and you then lose $**325.00** hard earned dollars. **Do the work.** Be sure that your proposed mark is not already out there. Even if it is somewhat close, you may have a problem, so don't do a lack luster job. **Search it out. Take a day or two to really search it out. Do the preliminary work before you file.** There is no need to lose your hard earned money. If it is already out there, then simply go back to the drawing board. I don't know about you, but I would rather have a **UNIQUE NAME** for a brand new venture that I came up with rather than a name that I **constantly** had to look **over my shoulder** because it is too similar to another name already in use.

6.   In a case like **Kidz** that is called a **Pseudonym** and it refers to a Trademark that sounds the same but uses a different unorthodox method of spelling. **Kidz** is not a proper way to spell Kids but if identified properly, the alternative spelling is acceptable. You want to search for "This Exact Phrase" as well as any combination of your proposed name. You want to take the time to see what is already out there. You would be surprised how many times someone thinks they have come up with a unique name only to find that same proposed name waiting for them in the Trademark data base on **USPTO**. Keep in mind that you are looking for "Live Trademarks" in the **USPTO** database. The "Dead" marks have been abandoned by the original owner so they will not preclude you from being able to file for that Trademark.

7.   It is important to point out that you can apply for a trademark on-line www.uspto.gov and the website has step-by-step instructions concerning the filing. In my book, **Low Cost Empire – Getting Down To Business – Filing Your First Trademark, I go over the entire process with you from beginning to end with a lot more insight**. If you have a brand new business and have not sold any goods or services across state lines then you can file what is called an "**Intent to Use**" Trademark Application. If from the moment you started your business you have been selling **interstate** (commerce between states), whether it is goods or services, then you can file an "**In Use**" Trademark Application. Again, these applications have built-in instructions. The filing fee is $325.00.

8.   If you have filed an intent to use application, once your mark is deemed by the trademark examiner to be worthy of being granted, you then have 5 chances to renew your Intent to Use status (6 month increments) before you must convert the status to IN USE or else you must forfeit the mark. When you do convert over to an In Use application that will cost you $100.00. Note: If you initially file as In Use and submit your specimen from the start, you will have no reason to worry about the Intent to Use or the $100.00 dollar conversion fee. People who file the Intent to Use do so because they simply are not selling their item whether it be goods or services AS OF YET but they sure plan to.

9.   Once you file for a trademark you should be using the "™" symbol after your proposed name wherever and whenever you use it. The "™" symbol alerts people that although a Trademark has not yet been issued, it lets them know that you are claiming the name as yours and you are currently somewhere along the chronology of the Trademark Application process. If you are in the "service business" then use the "SM" superscripted after the name of your company or product name. When you are issued the Trademark and it

becomes Registered and is no longer just a pending application, you will then place a "®" at the end of the mark and you will make sure that it is on everything and everywhere that your name appears. The "®" symbol lets people know that the mark is your property, protected in all fifty states from infringement or unauthorized use.

10. **Some things to consider**: If you can add a tagline to your trademark it will help to make it even more unique. If there was an issue as to confusion of two similar marks, the trademark examiner will have an easier time in determining if there is such a conflict if your mark has a unique tagline. Some famous taglines are "Things go better with Coke", "Just do it" by Nike. Then we have the other aspect that people are filing more and more and that is the **sound mark** which another part of the overall trademark process. This will help to make your trademark even more distinctive. Some famous sound marks are NBC's three tones, Intel's 4 notes Most major production companies end TV shows with their sound marks. This is big business so be inventive and be creative. Make this naming process a fun and creative process.

11. You will be surprised how you can be your own marketing firm. On the subject of Trademark, another thing that you can do is to create your own terminology within your line of business. In this way, people start using your self created buzz words and just maybe some term you made up will become part of the jargon of that industry. You can coin your own terms and have people use your vocabulary. It is also serves to make others think that they are not up on something and they need to check out your site. Have fun with your concepts. Be creative and enjoy the process.

Take Note: It is important to point out that the name of your company and the logo of your company should *paint a picture or mood in one's mind concerning the mindset or feel of the company*. This goes for whether it is a name, logo or picture. In the name of the logo see if any of the letters can be substituted with an object such as in the Sopranos logo using a **gun** in place of the "r" or Louis Ellman's logo We Want You To Know where he uses an open book in place of a "w" in the word Know." On the left is a sample of the two trademarks.

Next Step 2: Check on the availability of the proposed name as a **domain name, also known as URL (Universal Resource Locator) and/or website name for availability**.

Domain Names

Let's talk about the domain name aspect. You know that when you start a business, you need to have a domain name. You will need a website because people sort of take it for granted that you should have one if you are running a business. So, where do we go to purchase a domain name? There are many places that sell domain names. If you buy a domain name from **company A** and you hook up with a website hosting company which I will call **company B,** you can point your domain name residing on the server of one hosting company to the server location of another hosting company if necessary.

Why would you have to point to another company? Well, I will give you a good example. Let's say you already own a particular domain name. You buy a website from a hosting company that sells template websites or you use the free version. Your domain name is under godaddy.com and your website is from let us say **Webs.com** or **Weebly.com** which are free website companies for the most part. I say for the most part simply because for about $5.99 a month, you don't get the little commercials on the side. So, in order to use your domain name that is under the control of godaddy.com, you can simply point your domain elsewhere so that you can use the website you developed at another hosting site. I usually buy my domains from godaddy.com. They have low prices (at this point $11.99-14.99 for the whole year and web hosting from under a hundred dollars for the whole year). There are other lower cost domain name providers but they may or may not have the same amount of support that Godaddy has. I also make use of **fatwallet.com** where you can get numerous coupons for godaddy so that you pay less for all of your domains usually in the 20% range.

We have used godaddy.com in most cases because of their offerings and services. Keep in mind that if you have domain names with other services you can always transfer them to the hosting company of your choice. All hosting companies have provisions to allow you to transfer your domain names to the hosting company of your choice. It is a lot easier to keep track of your domains names if they are all in one place.

So we go to godaddy.com in order to look up our proposed domain name.

I put in my proposed name and pray.....

✔ **JOHNNYONENOTE.COM is available!**

Check the domain names that you would like to register below.
▶ Why you need multiple domains
▶ View options & pricing

?	.com*	.info*	.net*	.org*	.me	.mobi*	.us
Select All	☑ $9.99/yr save!	☐ BEST VALUE! $0.89 save $9.80!	☐ SALE! $8.99/yr save $4.00!	☐ $14.99/yr	☐ $19.99/yr	☐ $7.99 save $7.00!	☐ SPECIAL! $4.99 save $15.00!

Okay: **Now it gets interesting**! If you look at the top of this picture it says that **johnnyonenote.com is available**. Okay great! It also alerts you to the other extensions that are also available under that name. We recommend that you grab extensions such as **.US, .BIZ, .INFO, .NET, .mobi, .TV and .Org** This will cost you a little money. This will protect you against other people using your proposed name by purchasing one of these other domain extensions that use your name.

The idea here is that you want to stop **others** from profiting on your name by using your name and simply using a different extension of the name. What if a rival does something underhanded such as putting out a site that says how you wronged them or how your product is bad or your service inadequate. What if they did so using an extension that you could have easily purchased so that **it was not available** for this purpose. This would then leave you frustrated that you just didn't buy those URL's when you had the chance. People can damage your proposed name and reputation before you really even get started. This is all about locking up your name in the internet world and this is a vital step that we do for ourselves and anyone else that we deal with in terms of our AdvanceTo business services. It is also noteworthy that **.US** is for the United States and any trademark owner should own the **.US** URL of the trademark they own. This little exercise that we just went through is a **very important step** and should not be minimized in its importance.

If you wait to lock up the name (your name, your identity), as we suggested, you will regret it because when people come across something they like they might buy all of the available domains and then they are in the **driver's seat**. Don't let anyone hijack your name! Buy them up and protect your name and discourage these people who just look to get in on a good thing.

Note: If you look up a proposed domain name that you want and find that it is already secured by someone else, you may wish to know who actually owns the name and when they bought it. Every web hosting company has a place on their site called **"WHO IS"**. The *Who Is* database will let you know 1) who they are, (provided that they did not subscribe to a domain name proxy service that protects the name and address of the actual owner) 2) where they are from, 3) when they bought the domain and 4) when it expires. You may wish to keep track and see if that person renews the domain. If not, you can at that point make the attempt to purchase it. Our advice is do not let any one name hang you up and stop your progress. Some people who buy URL's also purchase the proxy service that protects a person from knowing the actual name and address of the owner of the domain name.

If you have a business where you don't want to have someone find out your personal address you owe it to yourself to use the **Domains By Proxy** service when you purchase your domains. There is an additional fee for this service but privacy is very important to certain individuals that do not want to have people knocking on their door unexpectedly. If you have a site where your picture is posted on the site and you live at the place indicated in the **"Who Is"** listing, you should consider the **proxy service** for your protection and privacy.

Once you buy the domains you can **activate the ".com"** domain extension, which will allow you to start your low cost website hosting plan and will give you your e-mail address as well. One good thing about godaddy.com is that the control panel is easy to navigate and it is easy to set your e-mail address which can be used right away. Other low cost options for hosting are webs.com and weebly.com.

Remember, for quick to learn template sites you can go to **freewebs.com and weebly.com** which have a very easy template program to get you up and running in no time.

Next Step 3: We also immediately check on the availability of the **concept name** for corporate availability. Keep in mind that if the name is not available in your state to use as a corporate name you can incorporate in another state such as the ever popular "Delaware Corporation" or the "Nevada Corporation", but you will need to find the filing service that deals with establishing a corporate residence. These are known as **Registered Agents**. So, for example, in Delaware go to **http://corp.delaware.gov** to get a listing of those agents that can help establish your corporate residence. Virtually all states require corporations, limited liability companies (LLC), nonprofits, limited partnerships (LPs) and limited liability partnerships (LLPs) formed or foreign qualified there to have a registered agent in the state. The Registered Agent must have a physical presence and address (no P.O. Boxes allowed) and must be available during normal business hours.

The **registered agent** is responsible for receiving important legal and tax documents on behalf of the business. Service of Process (sometimes called notice of litigation), which is the document that initiates a lawsuit, is served to the registered agent for a business. Proper handling of and timely response to this document are vital, as not doing so can result in significant adverse consequences to the business. Additionally, the registered agent often receives mail and tax documents from the state on behalf of business. Timely handling of these documents is also important as states typically impose deadlines for annual report and franchise tax payments. They are not expensive (up to

$150.00) per year depending on the service, but you have to have an "official location" in the State that you incorporate in even though you do not reside there.

It is important to note that these three items are now essential for doing business. **What is the significance of checking these three items**? If you want to operate both locally and globally then you are going to need to own the name of your company and have ownership and control of your trade name. Down the road, other people may become interested in a licensing agreement with you because they wish to use your name or logo on goods that they produce. Another possible avenue you may wish to explore is franchising. If you decide to ever go that route you will need to own your name.

By owning the name of your entity in terms of goods or services (your brand name), **people need your permission if they are to use that name on goods or services, which would amount to the formation of a licensing agreement**. A great book on licensing agreements for the lay person is **License Your Invention by Richard Stim**. This book goes over all the aspects of a license agreement and will give you a comfortable knowledge of the subject. *The importance of owning your concept name prevents others from using it without your permission as well allowing you to properly enter into franchise and licensing opportunities*. This is why you need to file for **trademark protection**. *IMPORTANT! READ*: The three items mentioned above (trademarks, domains, and corporations) are so inter-related that the following scenario(s) are possible:

You go to the Division of Corporations in your state and find that no one has your corporate name. **Great**! When you go to a hosting company or domain seller and look up the proposed name for a URL (domain name) it is possible that someone already has the **.com Now what!** My corporate name is open, but someone already has the **.com** under my proposed name. Well, they might have the **.com** but you can always grab the **.net or .biz** if they are available, etc. Although you didn't get **the coveted .com** at least you can still use your proposed name. Wait, it gets even better! Alright, we are clear for the corporation, we have a domain name available but when we look up the trademark to see the availability, someone already has the trademark and they are using it under the <u>**same classification**</u> **that you would have used it for**.

If this is the case, don't waste time trying to get around it. Take it as a sign to just come up with a different name. If there already is a person or entity (a company or corporation) owning an existing "live" or pending trademark under your proposed name they wield a lot of power and can make trouble for you. You will never be able to relax and enjoy your name knowing that someone else has beat you to the punch and is already using the name. After having spent a large sum of money in set-up, business cards, letterhead and the like, it's no fun being contacted by someone's attorney telling you to **cease and desist** immediately from using the name for threat of a lawsuit. If someone else already has the Trademark, it is recommended that you think up a new name. Chances are it will be **a lot** better. The idea is that you have a unique name owned by you **free and clear**.

Once you find the name that is **unique** in all three categories (*corporate, domain and trademark*) that is the one you want!! We cannot be more direct. Be inventive and come up with a unique name! If someone has the **.com** but they **don't** have the **corporation** or the **trademark**, go for the **.net**, **.biz**, **.US** and **.TV**, because at least the name can be protected in terms of trademark. Not having the **.com** is not the end of the world. Yes, you would rather have the **.com** as well but many well-known businesses have a domain name extension that is not a **.com** and they do fine. For those of you who are not in a position to afford a United States Trademark **consider doing a State Trademark** at first. At the very least you will have domain over others within your state in terms of the use of the mark. At a point down the road you can file for the United States mark which will then protect you in all 50 states. On each state's Official Website look for their state trademark section. Whew…what a business.

Just understanding *this section alone means that you would have learned much from this booklet and will now be better prepared to avoid problems resulting from not checking these items before moving ahead. This same scenario happens with inventors who don't bother to do patent searches thinking that their "New" invention is unique.*

Incorporation:

You check on the availability of the name for incorporation because you really **don't** want to operate under your **own name** if possible. The first reason for doing this is protection. The last thing that you want is for something to happen where one of your new customers has some kind of problem with your service or product and decides to sue you. Without the umbrella of a corporation they are **suing you personally** and not your corporation, which is a **separate entity**. In the worse case scenario, you may need to dissolve the corporation or declare bankruptcy if a large judgment is rendered against you. Like anything else, if you are careful in what you do and have procedures in place you most likely will never have these problems, but they do happen from time to time and you want to be protected. The other reason for incorporating is that you want to be able to take advantage of the write-offs allowed for your business, everything from supplies, meetings, equipment, car mileage, gas, discounts at stores when you give them your Tax ID number and it goes on. In addition, when you are incorporated, it helps lend to your credibility as a company and is more attractive on business cards and it places you on a more sophisticated level. Having a corporation also opens you up to **business lines of credit**. Visit **cashflowexperts.biz or the tomkishshow.com (Tom Kish) for expert help in attaining business lines of credit.**

How do you check if the name is available for incorporation?

You can check on your own state website for this information. Every state has its own **official state website**. As the owners of AdvanceTo, we live in New York and use the "Official New York State Website", which will be used as an example:

http://www.dos.state.ny.us/corp/corpwww.html

CORPORATIONS AND BUSINESS ENTITIES

- Mission
- Search Our Corporation/Business Entity Database Here
- Rules and Regulations of the Division of Corporations
- Legal Memoranda
  Doing Business in New York
  Formation of Business Entities

  FREQUENTLY ASKED QUESTIONS
  Business Corporations
  Not-for-Profit Corporations
  Limited Liability Companies
  Limited Partnerships
  Limited Liability Partnerships
  Biennial Statements for Corporations and LLCs and LLP Statement
  Updates for LLPs

  FILING INFORMATION, FORMS AND FEES
  Business Corporations
  Not-for-Profit Corporations
  Limited Liability Companies
  Limited Partnerships
  Limited Liability Partnerships

- Mission
- Search Our Corporation/Business Entity Database Here
- Rules and Regulations of the Division of Corporations
- Legal Memoranda

In the New York State site as an example, they have an area as shown above that has everything you could possibly do as it relates to incorporation. The "Search Our Corporation Database" section is important because this is where you get the chance to see if your **proposed name is available**. If you put your proposed name in and it comes up, then someone else has already secured that name. If that is the case don't be discouraged. Sometimes it is a sign from above that you should think of **another name** and many times (and it has happened to me) you end up coming up with an even **better** name than before.

Next, what type of corporation are you going to going to be? There are C-Corps, Limited Liability Corps., Sub Chapter S Corps., Personal Corps., Not-for-Profit Corps. and many more. In this booklet, you will be provided with an explanation of each one, but first, let's continue with discussion of the first step in incorporation. Once you decide upon your name, you would go to the part of the site in your state that provides the automated process to create your corporation. It should be noted that not all states have automated sites but still require that you send the paperwork to an address by mail. On the automated sites, as part of the overall process, you can also receive your new Tax I.D. (Identification Number) that same day as well as your **certificate of incorporation**, which you can print as well. Once you get your **certificate of incorporation** you can go to the bank with your **black book** (must have the black book), a loose leaf binder containing the ***minutes, by-Laws, customized Stock certificates, stock transfer ledger, metal corporate seal with company name*** (*if still required by your state most do not*). Many states no longer require the Corporate Seal. You can go to one of the many services that will prepare a Black Book. Your Black Book would include your **Certificate of Incorporation**, meeting forms, transfer of ownership of stock forms, etc. With your Certificate of Incorporation and your black book you would then open your **corporate bank account**.

You might even at this point, try to establish a line of credit for your new corporation by applying to one of the many credit card companies. The bank account will give your new company much needed credibility. When people want to pay you for your services they will now be making the checks out to **your corporate name**. If you pay for your Corporate Filing fee by money order or check, you send the form by mail to the address they give you and if I were you, I would do it by registered or certified mail, return receipt requested. If you are in New York State, you send the completed Certificate of Incorporation, together with the statutory filing fee of $135, to the Department of State, Division of Corporations, 41 State Street, Albany, NY 12231. Whatever state you happen to live in, your Official State Site will give you the information as to where to send payment for your New Corporation if not doing so by Credit or Debit Card. So, go to Google and type in Official State Site of (Your State) today!

Note: If you get credit for your new corporation take a 10-20% amount of the credit line and place it in the bank account and leave it in there. After 6 months, that untouched money will be viewed as a seasoned asset and will help you to establish even larger lines of credit.

The forms area of whatever state you live in will look somewhat similar in nature to the New York site. You just have to remember that you must go to your Official State Site!

FILING INFORMATION, FORMS AND FEES
Business Corporations
Not-for-Profit Corporations
Limited Liability Companies
Limited Partnerships
Limited Liability Partnerships

As promised, here are the different types of corporations and their meanings:

The following appeared on the **New York State website, Division of Corporations** link where a full explanation is given as to the differences between the different types of corporate entities that exist. This will be very helpful in having you see the **distinction** between the different types of corporations.

If you want to operate a **business corporation:**

- then you must *file* a Certificate of Incorporation (signed by at least one incorporator) *with* the Department of State.

- Personal liability is limited, for shareholders.

- The life-span of the business is perpetual; *or* for a designated period stipulated in the Certificate of Incorporation.

- For purposes of taxation a corporation pays state franchise taxes and taxes on income; shareholders pay taxes on income distributed as dividends (a limited exception exists for "Subchapter S" corporations). When it comes to Subchapter S corporations they are allowed to pass their losses though to the individual, so that they reduce their personal income. Subchapter S corporations were created in order to assist smaller corporations (with no more than 75 owners) the ability to off-set their losses against other income.

If you want to operate a **limited liability company:**

- then you must *file* Articles of Organization (signed by one or more organizers) *with* the Department of State.

- Personal liability is generally limited, although the Articles of Organization can specify that member(s) will be liable for company debts, etc.

- The life-span of the business may be for a designated period stipulated in the Articles of Organization; *or* until a dissolution event occurs and the company takes no action to continue.

- For purposes of taxation an LLC can elect its classification for federal tax purposes. An LLC with two or more members can elect to be an association (corporation) or a partnership; an LLC with one member can elect to be an association (corporation) or elect to be disregarded as an entity separate from its owner (in effect, to be treated as a sole proprietorship for federal tax purposes).

If you want to operate a **general partnership**:

- then you must *file* an Assumed Name Certificate (following an agreement of the partners) *with* the clerk of the county/ies in which the business is conducted.
- Personal liability is joint and individual for the general partners who are responsible for the obligations of the partnership.
- The life-span of the business is for a designated period stipulated in the partnership agreement; *or* until a dissolution event occurs.
- For purposes of taxation a general partnership is not treated as a separate taxable entity; business income is taxed through each general partner's personal tax return.

If you want to operate a **limited partnership**:

- then you must *file* a Certificate of Limited Partnership (following an agreement of the partners) *with* the Department of State.
- Personal liability is joint and individual for the general partners who are responsible for the obligations of the partnership; limited partners are liable to the extent of their capital contribution to the partnership.

The life-span of the business is for a designated period stipulated in the partnership agreement; *or* until a dissolution event occurs, subject to any right to continue that may be stated in the partnership agreement. The life span of the business might involve for example, a project that will last two years and after the period stated concerning this project is over then the partnership is no longer in effect.

- For purposes of taxation a limited partnership is not treated as a separate taxable entity; business income is taxed through each partner's personal tax return.

If you want to operate a **sole proprietorship**:

- then you must *file* an Assumed Name Certificate *with* the clerk of the county/ies in which the business is conducted *ONLY IF* you are operating under a name other than the proprietor's (no formation document is required).
- Personal liability is full- a sole proprietor is personally responsible for all debts of his or her business.
- The life-span of the business is determined by the individual (proprietorships automatically cease on the retirement or death of the sole proprietor).
- For purposes of taxation business income is reported and taxed through the sole proprietor's personal tax return.

The 3 Steps Essential Process For
New Concept Name Summation

1. The Business Plan is important but not for this talk in particular.. What do you bring to the market. How are you different? You can go to these places to obtain business plans: **Score.org – Under their "Templates and Tools" section they have business plan templates and Entreprenuer.com** www.entrepreneur.com/formnet/businessplantemplates.

2. **The 3 essential searches**. Must make sure that someone else does not already have the name or own it as a Trademark. This will just result in you receiving a letter down the line from an attorney telling you to cease and desist from using the name.

3. In order to check to see if your name is already being used by someone else in the line of business that you hoped to use it in go to: USPTO.gov site and go to the search trademarks feature and choose "**new user**" search and you search your proposed new business concept name.

4. If it comes up empty, great but you should also be searching for any of the terms related to the name. Anything a little too close will also result in a problem. If filed, the examiner could reject your application based on a prior filing that already uses the proposed mark. So first do your homework thoroughly or go to an attorney or a Trademark search service if you are not experienced.

5. Trademark protection: We can help you which will allow you to own your name and control your name in all fifty states. Anyone interested in using your trade name will have to come to you first and then both parties will work out what is called a Licensing Agreement which allows an entity to make use of your name for an agreed upon fee for a certain period of time. You may also wish to one day create a franchise and you will need to own the name in order to do so.

6. Step 2. Go to a domain hosting company such as godaddy.com and search for your proposed business name. If no one has it, it will say that it is available. It is recommended that you purchase as many of the domains as possible in order to prevent others from piggybacking on your name with other websites.

7. Remember you are trying to build a brand and the more you control of the name the better. The other domains that you purchase other than the .com **can be forwarded over to the .com** so they will not go to waste. Buying all these domains will probably cost you $100.00 dollars or less. Go to **Fatwallet.com** and look for sales for Godaddy for new domains. That will enable you to trim the bill quite a bit.

8. So far we are talking about controlling the Trademark and Domain aspect of your proposed name. Every time you come up with a new

name you should be going through this process of accessing the availability of the name in question.

9. What if someone already has the .com? If that entity did not file for Trademark Protection and you really love the name, then buy up all of the .domains that are available and monitor the .com extension to wait for your opportunity when you may be able to grab it. But at least you own the other domains and you can still run your business with that name.

10. Use the "**Who Is**" area next to the listed domain to know who owns the domain and when it is due for renewal. You can also go onto a list and if the owner does not renew then you can bid for it.

11. Keep in mind overall that if your original name does not work out for any reason, and you have to come up with another name the other name that you were forced to come up with is usually even better than the first one. If it is totally available you will know so because of the use of this 3 step process. Owning the name outright is your goal. So, I am a big fan of going back to the drawing board because it usually results in an even better name.

12. Step 3: The final step of the 3 step process is checking on the availability for Incorporation. If you go to Google and search for the Official State website for whatever state you wish to incorporate in. In the corporate section, it will let you search out the proposed corporate name for availability. Some states let you do the whole process on-line other states make you fill out a form and mail it in with payment. Once you incorporate, you then get your Federal Tax ID number and when you have your paperwork and black book you can then go to the bank and open a corporate account. AdvanceTo can help with your incorporation. We are very reasonable.

13. If you don't reside in the state in which you incorporate, then you will have to make use of a Registered Agent to establish an official corporate address. The Registered Agents for a particular state are listed on each individual state website. Registered agents provide for a fee an official corporate address where someone can send mail to you or serve papers if necessary. Cost will be from $75.00 - $125.00 dollars a year but you need an official address.

14. Because most of you will have multiple business ideas this 3 step process will always serve you. 1. Trademark search: if clean go to domains and buy up as many as you can and finally take care of incorporation. Knowing the trade name is under your control you can do business cards, letterhead etc. etc. Lock down the name, control the name. After all, it is your property.

15. Remember, there is no law stating that your Trademark name has to be the same as your Corporate name. My Trademark can be

Cool Sun while my Corporation can be **Idesign**. Get it? Good luck with everything!

16. If you want us to consult with you call us at 888-422-0692 Ext. 2 You can also contact me at www.lowcostempire.com

International Schedule of Classes of Goods and Services For A Trademark Filing – What Classification Does Your Business or Service Fall Under?

GOODS

1. Chemicals used in industry, science and photography, as well as in agriculture, horticulture and forestry; unprocessed artificial resins; unprocessed plastics; manures; fire extinguishing compositions; tempering and soldering preparations; chemical substances for preserving foodstuffs; tanning substances; adhesives used in industry.

2. Paints, varnishes, lacquers; preservatives against rust and against deterioration of wood; colorants; mordants; raw natural resins; metals in foil and powder form for painters, decorators, printers and artists.

3. Bleaching preparations and other substances for laundry use; cleaning, polishing, scouring and abrasive preparations; soaps; perfumery, essential oils, cosmetics, hair lotions; dentifrices.

4. Industrial oils and greases; lubricants; dust absorbing, wetting and binding compositions; fuels (including motor spirit) and illuminants; candles, wicks.

5. Pharmaceutical, veterinary, and sanitary preparations; dietetic substances adapted for medical use, food for babies; plasters, materials for dressings; material for stopping teeth, dental wax; disinfectants; preparations for destroying vermin; fungicides, herbicides.

6. Common metals and their alloys; metal building materials; transportable buildings of metal; materials of metal for railway tracks; nonelectric cables and wires of common metal; ironmongery, small items of metal hardware; pipes and tubes of metal; safes; goods of common metal not included in other classes; ores.

7. Machines and machine tools; motors and engines (except for land vehicles); machine coupling and transmission components (except for land vehicles); agricultural implements other than hand-operated; incubators for eggs.

8. Hand tools and implements (hand-operated); cutlery; side arms; razors.

9. Scientific, nautical, surveying, electric, photographic, cinematographic, optical, weighing, measuring, signalling, checking (supervision), life-saving and teaching apparatus and instruments; apparatus for recording, transmission or reproduction of sound or images; magnetic data carriers, recording discs; automatic vending machines and mechanisms for coin operated apparatus; cash registers, calculating machines, data processing equipment and computers; fire extinguishing apparatus.
10. Surgical, medical, dental, and veterinary apparatus and instruments, artificial limbs, eyes, and teeth; orthopedic articles; suture materials.
11. Apparatus for lighting, heating, steam generating, cooking, refrigerating, drying, ventilating, water supply, and sanitary purposes.
12. Vehicles; apparatus for locomotion by land, air, or water.
13. Firearms; ammunition and projectiles; explosives; fireworks.
14. Precious metals and their alloys and goods in precious metals or coated therewith, not included in other classes; jewelry, precious stones; horological and chronometric instruments.
15. Musical instruments.
16. Paper, cardboard and goods made from these materials, not included in other classes; printed matter; bookbinding material; photographs; stationery; adhesives for stationery or household purposes; artists' materials; paint brushes; typewriters and office requisites (except furniture); instructional and teaching material (except apparatus); plastic materials for packaging (not included in other classes); playing cards; printers' type; printing blocks.
17. Rubber, gutta-percha, gum, asbestos, mica and goods made from these materials and not included in other classes; plastics in extruded form for use in manufacture; packing, stopping and insulating materials; flexible pipes, not of metal.
18. Leather and imitations of leather, and goods made of these materials and not included in other classes; animal skins, hides; trunks and travelling bags; umbrellas, parasols and walking sticks; whips, harness and saddlery.
19. Building materials (non-metallic); nonmetallic rigid pipes for building; asphalt, pitch and bitumen; nonmetallic transportable buildings; monuments, not of metal.
20. Furniture, mirrors, picture frames; goods (not included in other classes) of wood, cork, reed, cane, wicker, horn, bone, ivory, whalebone, shell, amber, mother-of-pearl, meerschaum and substitutes for all these materials, or of plastics.
21. Household or kitchen utensils and containers (not of precious metal or coated therewith); combs and sponges; brushes (except paint brushes); brush-making materials; articles for cleaning purposes; steel-wool; unworked or semi-worked glass (except glass used in building); glassware, porcelain and earthenware not included in other classes.

22. Ropes, string, nets, tents, awnings, tarpaulins, sails, sacks and bags (not included in other classes); padding and stuffing materials (except of rubber or plastics); raw fibrous textile materials.
23.Yarns and threads, for textile use.
24. Textiles and textile goods, not included in other classes; beds and table covers.
25. Clothing, footwear, headgear.
26. Lace and embroidery, ribbons and braid; buttons, hooks and eyes, pins and needles; artificial flowers.
27. Carpets, rugs, mats and matting, linoleum and other materials for covering existing floors; wall hangings (non-textile).
28. Games and playthings; gymnastic and sporting articles not included in other classes; decorations for Christmas trees.
29. Meat, fish, poultry and game; meat extracts; preserved, dried and cooked fruits and vegetables; jellies, jams, fruit sauces; eggs, milk and milk products; edible oils and fats.
30. Coffee, tea, cocoa, sugar, rice, tapioca, sago, artificial coffee; flour and preparations made from cereals, bread, pastry and confectionery, ices; honey, treacle; yeast, baking powder; salt, mustard; vinegar, sauces (condiments); spices; ice.
31. Agricultural, horticultural and forestry products and grains not included in other classes; live animals; fresh fruits and vegetables; seeds, natural plants and flowers; foodstuffs for animals; malt.
32. Beers; mineral and aerated waters and other nonalcoholic drinks; fruit drinks and fruit juices; syrups and other preparations for making beverages.
33. Alcoholic beverages (except beers).
34. Tobacco; smokers' articles; matches.

SERVICES

35.	Advertising; business management; business administration; office functions.
36.	Insurance; financial affairs; monetary affairs; real estate affairs.
37.	Building construction; repair; installation services.
38.	Telecommunications.
39.	Transport; packaging and storage of goods; travel arrangement
40.	Treatment of materials.
41.	Education; providing of training; entertainment; sporting and cultural activities.
42.	Scientific and technological services and research and design relating thereto; industrial analysis and research services; design and development of computer hardware and software; legal services.
43.	Services for providing food and drink; temporary accommodations.
44.	Medical services; veterinary services; hygienic and beauty care for human beings or animals; agriculture, horticulture and forestry services.
45.	Personal and social services rendered by others to meet the needs of individuals; security services for the protection of property and individuals.

www.ingramcontent.com/pod-product-compliance
Lightning Source LLC
Chambersburg PA
CBHW081419170526
45166CB00010B/3408